The Dedalus Press
editor John F Deane

DOSTOEVSKY'S GRAVE

SELECTED POEMS

by

LELAND BARDWELL

 DEDALUS

THE DEDALUS PRESS
24 The Heath
Cypress Downs
Dublin 6W

ISBN 0 948268 91 3 (paper)
ISBN 0 948268 92 1 (bound)

Acknowledgements: to Bernard and Mary Loughlin for their
hospitality, and to "Cyphers", "Poetry Ireland Review",
"Arena", "Broadsheet", "Force 10"

Clóchur: Peanntrónaic Teo., 49 Br Crannach, BÁC 14

Cover Painting: Ruined Church at Confey, by Eileen Ferguson

The Dedalus Press receives financial assistance from
An Chomhairle Ealaíon, The Arts Council, Ireland.

CONTENTS

for my four sons
and two daughters,
William, Anna, Jacky,
Nicholas, Eddie, and John

Lea – land –   there was no shelter there;
no shelter from the cutting North.
So she went North into the brume.
For a while the new broom swept clean
but then the ashes of her bed
soon turned to rust.
And there was cold.
The earth was a frozen lump.
North again she went into the further
doom where the map ends
and she remembered the South
where the strollers were
like Mandarin figures on a Chinese silk;
"Have I come too far?" she asked
an old man making masks.
But he was waspish and unkind;
he answered not but pointed with skinny hand
to Lea – land –   there was no shelter there.

HOUSEWIFE

They filled in the halo
with chalk
a better picture, this,
they thought
(for she's no saint.)
They put pebbles on her nipples
to weigh them down.

She feigned patience;
  she waited,
    waited,
      waited.

Occasionally, during the waiting period
she came up with a small truth
while sweeping the dust
off the bread; at first
there was fruit, and left-overs
to finish up; soon
the water even was gone,
and money was everything.

Then the panther came
and sat on her lap.
His paws created a diversion
as soft as mushrooms on her thighs.

They tried to send her away
but she sat still.
(They knew there'd be a toll
for her returning)
But that would be later
much later.

She was crouching now,
her breasts lay naked on her ribs
like cotton gloves,

her legs had got like daffodil stalks
but her eyes were still angry.

The panther had gone.

The only way she knew this
was by the tone of their voices.

The way they could tell she was still there
was by the noise of the cupboard doors
being opened and shut.
She must be looking for something
they said.

FOR PAUL AND NESSA ON THE OCCASION OF THEIR MARRIAGE

Apart they tore the ropes asunder
and clearing the decks, each
cast a net in his own turbulent mind;
there revealed a high solitude
as equivocal as a war to end wars;
cast again for certainty, and found
memories old as an ill-tuned drawing room piano;
cast again for beauty and found
the petals of asters
each petal as thin
as a strand of the future.

They shall weave with the petals of asters
the skin of a shirt.

THEY PUT A BED IN THE PASSAGE
(On first looking into St. Pat's.)
for John Jordan

They put a bed in the passage
and said "lie down."
Glory glory glory
to the spring, not this side
of Thomas Street.
For we don't believe in flowers.

They gave us the dark side of the moon
to live upon
and not content with that
they quartered it till
it looked like a bad banana.
There we clung together
as far apart as possible
till the others came.
They brought ichor in their syringes
these dark venal furtive earth-men
and we admired them
like we admired Messrs. Stafford, Young and Cernan
but we didn't envy them.

For they shall return whence they came
like landlords who get no rent.
We promised to pay the rent
and we believed it. But we didn't do it.

That's why they kept coming back.

SAILOR SONG
i.m. Commander Robert Cooper

My great uncle Bob went French
and spoke of *Naufrages*
- he had traded sailors like silk
in foreign parts.
He showed me "Beetlejuice"
the brightest of all Orion's mates.

   The night sky spins on the lever
   the mariners love – it's a nervous sea
   The Leeward Islands lift and dip
   the sailors are braced by a nip of rum.
   Is it spikenard that wafts through the smothering fog?
   (The seabed lifts as the cormorants dive.)

With the drift of years the waves
must have arched their backs to flatter
the sailor who scanned his vegetable plot,
the furcoated caterpillar swung
on the cabbage leaf.
(The Red Admiral pinned to the box
was a butterfly hoax.)
It was strange that an old old man should have jet black hair.

   I feared that he would fall or drop
   a priceless porcelain jar _ I feared
   he would trip on the crusty stair
   and a carved wood head would bounce and chip
   but I never feared that he would die.

Only part of the heart's equipped
for a legacy of empty rooms –
a telescope to read the sky,
the lingering camphor smell
in the empty butterfly box.

HUSBANDS

My first husband hated intelligent women
he thought they were like avocado pears,
expensive, tasteless.

He said if I was let loose
I might go to Mexico
although his horizons
were leather skirts.

My second husband hated Mexicans
and me. He said we had ended the transfer.
He liked Antonioni women
with short hair and big bums
and wanted to be one.

I'd like a new one with no hatreds
and superb teeth
Both my husbands had grey smiles
and were transvestites.

I thought that stupid
(so what if my breasts
are like two fried eggs?)
They haven't any.

I was once screwed in Euston Station
and saw mercury running.
If I could have bottled it
I'd have made a fortune.

ON BEING SHUT OUT OF DESMOND O'GRADY'S
FLAT IN THE SMALL HOURS

Was it for this we crossed the Rubicon
(the crazy monk on roller skates)
Dove il scuola Athenaeum?
(A thousand Japs in the Vatican)

Amor dapis means *amor lacrimarum*
Legal organic high –
(There are nettles by the Tiber
they are wet, they sting.)
Non sunt fiori
And thou shalt weep
upon the water.

With the small annoyances of dawn –
a lost key –
il Professore sleeps
with his halo askew.

We'll play periferal giants
and tell half the story

WIFE WAITS FOR HUSBAND

Why do you come wine-dressed
with your whisky kisses
and throw back my curtain
wanting my ripples?

I do not lie corsetted
there is no toll-gate
come crazy come weary
but do not come wine-dressed
with your whisky kisses

turn over tiredly turn
   the bed over
tell me I'm whoring
tell me I'm wrong
but don't come with
tresses don't come with weeds
the dandelion clock
is the maker of seeds

he loves me he loves me
he loves me not lately

but do not come wine-dressed
from botchy night glories
do not come wine-dressed
with mother made stories

come with the whisky
and give me to drink
the future is fox-glove
it's poison it's poison
but poppy will soften
the lines on my street.

INISBOFIN

Mikey's eyes see further than the long sea
    in the short bar.
If an island is another land it isn't Ireland
and the islanders' insulated laugh is a valediction
    that no partings fathom.

Yet we return again and again
    as the pleated sea swells
to allow ourselves that moment of joy
as the Melody docks, the crafty old engines
    grinding to a halt
And Mikey's cagey welcome, small drops of merriment
    waltzing in the irises
would make the twelve bens bow down in salutation.

His brother Christy rests athwart the bows
    (he never smiles)
His salt lips are dried by his daily death
    banging from port to port with cargo and caution
His melody is the song he sings when the sun
    dips over the island's spine.

The rest of the crew, Young Jim, in his forty years
    a stranger to both, harbours his eyes
    like the skin of the bog where the sun runs like a scythe,
languid and orderly in his labour he hurls
    the Guinness kegs on the harbour tip
Short shrift for the returning vagrants
    fron Kensal Rise or Ealing West
or the Johnnie-come-latelies like ourselves
    gratefully settled like plovers on motionless ground
while the crowd disperses and the island, a figure of eight
    subsides once more in its ocean bed.

Mikey, stately in his sixty years
    drifts to Day's Bar, leaving the future behind him.

AN AFTERNOON WITH THE ARTIST
AT THE QUINN CLUB
for Gerry Mangan

Pat Quinn is the plenipotentiary
of compassion – like the blue whale
he puffs and gurgles – gurgles and puffs
while the cloves of hot spirit
cluster his lips he spreads vines
on the tampered marrow-skin
the monastery of his seventh child.

The dusk made a twist of lemon in a furtive sky
damp winter settled on the Wicklow night
sealed the little episodes of mud
with slate thin ice – the children repaired
with effortless confusion
to the thud of the pin-ball tables.

Free mandarin roots for all
roll up somnambulists, the empire is yours
we are the great sharers
something for all the family.
The ticket man has braced his varicose heart
has adopted a surgeon's smile
He knows the camels of fortune
don't come to poets. When the knees
swell and mottle like turnips
they'll yell for the knife.

The artist drinks his vodka straight –
we toast – all centuries combine –
the supreme and wide dominion –
the year of the Tiger.

We listen carefully to the cushions.

INISBOFIN (THE ROUE)

In the hot roar of Murray's bar
the roue stares lustfully
the old trench-coat hardened
like asbestos
– catch as catch can –
on the way to the toilet

We're crazy about this place
of wild mint and garlic
imagine poems can solve everything
grow into the landscape
like the surface turf
or like adding polish to a shoe

But the roue is there
sanding his lust in the blind way
we trip in ruts on a moonless night
if he goes home empty
with his limping dog
we lie untouched
among the nameless grave stones.

MOTHER SAID IT WOULD BE ALL RIGHT
WHEN FRANCIS CAME

Mother said it would be all right
when Frances came

Since the consumption took Rose
those roses on her cheeks,
mother said, meant T.B.

But it would be all right
when Frances came

And those fungi
camping in corners
and the case of the dead bat
in the meat safe
yes it would be all right
when Frances came.

Mother said, we must impress Frances
clean up the kitchen, make all ship shape
so I dressed up like All Hallows Eve
and Frances came.

She came and swept through
the house like Dracula
she raped us, drew blood
satin red and smooth
She was a volcano
and lava ran unstinted
over furnishings and beds
and carpets squirmed and floundered
as if the Lough Ness monster
lurked beneath them.

She scoured the buildings,
the barn, the cowshed,
she ravished the grass

between the cobbles in the yard
like she was shaving an old man's
chin for the sacrament.

I hid. I hid in the grease
of the chestnut tree. I hid
in the elbow of the laurel
I hid in the maw of the bran
barrel. I put on my lemon dress
and lay in a field of buttercups
and Frances came.

I gathered strength
and turned my art to the darkened well
over the hill of Confey
I scooped and scraped off the viscous scum
where all life teemed in miniature
I built a temple under the lichened stone
like a father's purse where all wealth
teems in miniature
and Frances came.

Mother said it would be all right
when Frances settled down

Although she cooked like
a German General, attacked
the bright red lumps of meat
as if they were Jews, Mother said
it would be all right
when Frances settled down

I cradled my terror
hid my obstinacy
and Mother screamed: Lunacy
Frances is a jewel

I had to agree at night
when God came down and kicked
the chamber pot at the foot of my bed
I had to kneel and pray
for yeast that would rise my soul
like Christmas cake
but my soul went off like kettle steam
I tried to call it back
It was Aladdin: New souls for old
and Frances came

It's the fever, she said
as she sat like dough
on the foot of my bed
You see, mother said
it's all right now.
When the fever went I could rise
from bed, provided I dressed up warm
and avoided draughts.

I tramped the house
like a tiddly-wink I jumped
from squares into pots
I was my best toy dog
and straw came out of my chest
I was Minnie Mouse in Mother's
high-heeled shoes
But Frances owned my soul

"In safe keeping," she said
and her ice-berg head
jerked widely and wisdom
snorted through her nose

Now I must pray to Frances
go on my knees at night

because Frances held my soul
between her fists like a rubber ball

But one day
one duck-egg-coloured day
Frances leaned out of the window
she leaned out and spoke
to the air like a racial memory

I stood in all this speaking
silent behind Frances
I basked in this and I was
secret as a wasp crawling into the jam

Frances was now lady-God
lady-God resting, and I was
lady-God's toy into which
she could replace my soul
like a key into a walking doll

But I was unwound and rubber
If she turned round and put her hand
on my stomach I'd say "Ma ma".

But I knew there was more to God
than just Frances. There must be proof
right inside Frances. So I crept nearer
I was moonsilence, I was rumpelstiltskin
hiding my name
and I was unguessable, I lifted
up Frances' skirt
and flung it over her head.

You will soon be a big girl,
Mother said, and there are things
you'll learn about then.

I won't beat you limp
like a rabbit-skin but what a pity
now that everything was so ship shape
that Frances had to leave.

I swallowed my soul
and it went down like a raw potato
when Mother had seen to this
she told me that there was a girl
in the village called Myra.
Pity she's an R.C., Mother said
but it would be all right
when Myra came.

OUTSIDE THE ODEON CAMDEN TOWN

The snow on the street like stewed apple
the buses slopslopping past
with carton-loads of paddies.
In the illuminated cheek-bones of the Odeon
cinema
on my twentyninth birthday I waited.

An aeroplane took off in Arizona
and Buddy Holly died.

Last week, Elvis Presley
felt his chest grip the skin – felt
his shrivelled parts like an empty money belt
quiver for the last time.

I am not weeping for an old star's death
or a man stumbling in secrecy
to an appointment with a mediocre end
but myself gone forty nine with memories
of my first record-player and a bunch
of "forty-fives" and a Greek boy
separating air from vowels

"Will you come... ba...by... will you come?"

BEFORE GOING UP

Before going up
she downed a pint of cooking sherry

How was it, she asked afterwards.

Good, he said, for you?

Fine.

FIRST

A dog should die outside, the others said
but I had taken her
scrunched up in my arms,
hidden her in the shed.

We lay together in a shroud of hay
holding death aside
like the curtain in a theatre.
But then it came: the blood.
It spurted from her mouth,
spurted on the flagstones
like a string of beads.

What follows obliterates,
with each new loss,
that accident of grief.
But how can one forget what was one's
first. First anything, first love,
first loss, first kiss.

CRYBABY

For John McLachlan

Her neighbours talked
with wasps in their teeth:
We heard your baby crying,
crying half the night.

Sweet chain of love, she shouted
that binds me to my child.

(She was at a party down the road
the night the host hanged himself.)

SNOW LOVE

Dublin is not accustomed
to this thick white coat
It has crept back into silence
in a cemetery of time

With the crack of the clock
the traffic starts; slow splashing
wheels make newly furrowed lines
filthy beneath this creaking skin
while day hangs up the sun
like a plug of orange tobacco.

We are happy to be ritually forgotten
lucky to belong to this great
redundant mass on this cold day.
To be free to count each others bones
beneath the bedclothes.

That wheeling spectacle beyond the glass
has all our sympathy, by God!
But we are free to make – repeat –
a blessing of each bone

Till the short day melts
like a candle in its saucer
and snow peters down once more
like silent falling stars.

HOW MY TRUE LOVE AND I LAY
WITHOUT TOUCHING

How my true love and I lay without touching
How my hand journeyed to the drumlin of his hip
my pelvis aching
Just like two saints or priests or nuns
my true love and I lay without touching.

How I would long for the brush of a kiss
to travel my cheek or the cheek of my groin
my heart aching
But just like two saints or priests or nuns
my true love and I lay without touching.

Last night in my dreams I spoke with his wife
his true love who had left him surely as they lay without
touching
my heart for her was aching
For like two saints or priests or nuns
the two loves once lay without touching

But the dream of her faded before concentrating
each to each in our innocent mutual hating
her hand aching
to blind me with bullets to prevent herself from pining
for a once love she longed for and lay without touching.

Now my true love lies in the mutton of madness
"I was always troubled by sex," he says, with great sadness
his wife and I aching
in our cold single beds with many seas dividing
as we think of the years we spent without touching.

FROM A PAINTING BY ARTEMESIA GENTILESCHI

How strange to be wielding this knife
with such violence
Regard the bounce of muscle on my arms
between my fingers the scarlet beads
of victory.

Who is beneath my bloodied hand
(If they name me wanton then I am
as is he between my nimble fingers)
But for convenience I have named him Holofernes
and she? The woman hacking off his head?
I call her Judith (how pretty in comparison
her hand maid – assistant in this direful deed
Great gentle hands – the midwife
hovering over the labour bed.)

I do not pierce my breast with thorns
the red rose has no song for me.
(Rose – white my bosom – pure –
clean as foam on the crest of a wave.
I cleanse my pallette with this violent act.)
Later I shall paint the humble, the heroic.

CHAIN STROKES

The breathing began at eight p.m.
Two starched nurses – angry swans –
In my head the sonata – B flat minor –
That was my sleep
Restless chromatic quavers.

I awoke
Lento. Again lento.

She died at eight a.m.

Ten years later
I read *Sons and Lovers*.

EXILES

for Geraldine O'Reilly

Those were the seedlings we sowed
pricked and primed against the hard
rocks of poverty.

Those were the seedlings –
we have put names on their
children. The children
of Gurlay Flynn and Mother Jones –
Oh your america

Tumbletown and Dead River Valley
Famine-forced they crowded the canals
from the bog of Allen to Idaho
Crossed the Atlantic
in the stench of homelessness.

Now Bridie, don't forget to say your prayers.

Mother, get me a bride
from out the four green fields –
my fields.

Mean fields.

Some hid behind the lace
others shed stone tears
Useless tears.

To Hell with the bleeding fingers
of all the women
(A nickel a day, make hay make hay)
Cooking fat at night
in the quiver of the candle.

We'll show you who the boss is,
you Irish bitches.

Now Bridie, keep your legs crossed
And the rosary between your toes.

But they rose... rose
like bonfires on a mountain,
every mansheila of them
rose against the whips
broke files, made unions
It was a slow going –
a slow coming.

Dear Bridie, I received the dollars.
Your father's taken ill
I got shoes for Peadar
and Kathleen.
I'll put the rest by.
Pray for me.

Why are we waiting?
Give me the D.C.9
New York, New World
New suitcase, transit visa.

Uncle Tom, find me a husband
and a Green Card
and I'll never leave
your america.

My Green Card

Mean Card.

This is your pilot
pointing pilot
Feathering down on Kennedy Airport

Oh America!

I strike out now
in a skyscrape of desire
quivering for dollars.
You mean I've come all the way from Clontarf
and there's no job?

Why is everyone sleeping
in the subway?

These are the seedlings we sow
pricked and primed against
the hard rocks of poverty

We put names on these children
the children of Gurlay Flynn
and Mother Jones

Oh your america.

REMEMBERING THE BLINDNESS OF
JORGE LUIS BORGES

He went off last year
to – I hope – some far-seeing place
At that fearsome Taoiseach do
I took his quilted hand
barely murmuring how honoured
I was to meet him
With Byronic irony he muttered
So is everyone else.

De donde viene este vino?
In that dark world
we were invisible accomplices
bandits without a cause
banderillos without a bull.

Penumbra – shadow – poet of eternal light.

BREACH BABY

Black panther, he does not
streak through forests.
Back and forth, back and forth
in this house of his.
In this house of his, he paces.

My son who is gone five –
the solitary watcher –
says quietly:

He does not know which way.

He remembers my rib-cage.

POINTLESS

You go on and on.

But imagine the world without music.
Just imagine – no fifths, no thirds,
no arpeggios, no atonal notes.
(And surely God invented the octave.)

I once saw a horse dance in Phoenix Park.

Yes you go on and on
saying art, unless political, is pointless
But you don't pick blackberries with me
you are not interested in mud.

CLONDALKIN CONCRETE

Late again! You know we keep regular hours
in Clondalkin Concrete.

I was the Temp.
The one who worked from five past nine till six
with no let up
But they kept regular hours at Clondalkin Concrete

From Clondalkin Concrete I wrote a letter to Paul
I told him I was writing concrete verse
and very soon I would send them, block on clock
in Clondalkin Concrete we keep stanzas
numbered and counted carefully, cement and sand
We keep regular poems in Clondalkin Concrete

All the while I worked in Clondalkin Concrete
I must have sold a million tons of blocks
I was a bungalow blitz of a typist
Invoice neat in my work
But I wrote, Dear Paul, I dedicate to you
every block of a concrete stanza
every freezing grain of sand
For I'm up to my neck in Clondalkin Concrete

While directly gazing into my boss's watery studs
All that Fall, I shouted, All that Fall

MOTH DUST

Pumpkin fond pumpkin
had water under the chin
It didn't matter.
It didn't matter then, until
his eyes became two asterisks
his back a scythe
and with his dainty fingers
he filled my mouth with sloes
my mind with moth dust.

But he left Mahommed's thumbprint
on my shoulder.

CHILDREN'S GAMES
for William and Anna Bardwell

Once upon a time
I saw my two children playing
where Karl Marx was lying
with a tombstone on his head;
they were naked from the waist down

and the English around and around said
Better the children dead
than naked from the waist down

Now I was a foreigner
on that cold Highgate Hill
but I bore no ill to the English
no ill

So I toiled away by the Spaniards
where the English were all lovers
and their legs gleamed O
so cold and naked
naked from the waist down

and I tried another graveyard
and found another plot
where Sigmund Freud was lying
in his eiderdown of weeds

My children, I said, romp away
this little strip is yours
for the dead are mostly idle
and do not care if you are naked
naked from the waist down

and the graves began to smile
and the hymn of England fade
and my children took out their pocket knives
and carved on the limey stone:

Dr Freud lies here in the nettles
we are dancing on his head

HER SISTER'S CHILD

Her sister's child is sleeping with her husband
and she is not a bit surprised.
He loved her far too much to stake his all,
(he said); she's not so sure,
the baby leaves his bed at five.

Her sister's child is blonde and bonnie and blithe,
at twenty-one a little immature
(perhaps a little indiscreet?)
should be more circumspect, you'd think.

   When she is far away
   and still alive she'll tell
   this story with more subtlety.

AFTER PUSHKIN

A pinch of laughter opened up his face
"Irish?" he said. "Ireland!"
"What do you do there really?"
With O a wave of nonchalance, "You know" I said
"Write poems, books, you know, that sort of thing –
Waste a lot of trees..."

A ring of comprehension, "Rabbie Burns" he said.
"Ah no, that other lot – O'Casey, Joyce –
A different kettle of Celtic fish"

"I see" he said, his tiny specs
transparent flowers of recognition
"The Portrait, him I know, I like him much –
I just stamp passports"

I had stepped across his threshold
from this pin in the Atlantic
and placed my brief amongst the idols
and the pictures – Akhmatova, Osip and Nadezda –
The Rubens, Caravaggios, Matisses –
All histories combine – and he
who takes no part in this idiot
warp and woof of words
gazes at me sternly from his window,
nodding, sees how turning in a circle
everything comes round.

MEMORY

I remember my mother who hated onions
sex and mongrel dogs,
my father's rusty fingers
wading through butterflies.
So I grew to talk kindly with enemies,
soldiers and policemen.
I stare into the morphine of memory
pressing the needle into the weakest spot.

I wonder does she hold her skirt around her knees
in the heaven she believed in,
the demon sex beaten to a dish-cloth
with semi-colons of thou shalt nots
full stops of self abasement
or does she lie, legs splayed out
for dogs and pictures and others to enter her
face glazed in anticipation
for something she never experienced before.

Last week I visited her grave
a dead wreath had landed askew the weathered cross.
Good day, Ma, I said and lifted the crumbling crown
and hurled it into the fields of Confey.

ON MISTAKING A JESUIT LECTURE FOR A POETRY READING

Is this the poetry reading?
Shh... all heads turn in my direction.
I settle down beside a balding man
and listen to the speaker.
He tells of Paris, nineteen eighty eight
of how the doors are open every day
I wait to hear how poets have been entertained
and housed and watered freely
but not a word of verse or stanza
crutch or limp is coming from his lips.
This is a long long intro, think I
looking at the man whose rim of hair
is tonsure like
(but surely tonsures have gone out, think I)
he sneers unfriendlily, I draw my breath
uncross my knees, look round for the three poets
I came to hear. No poet. No familiar face
and then the awful truth!
I am the only woman in the place.
Ahem, I mutter through my tonsils
Where do you think I am?
A howl of shhishes echoes from the ashtray walls
Mr Tonsure very nearly spits.
Now my buttocks are experiencing the sting
of tensing muscles – my knee has gone to sleep
I dare not move. I feel like shouting "Fire"
or anything that might get me out
but everything's against me, doors are closed
no doubt I am locked in. Perhaps I'm dead
and this is where the wretched sinners
go – to poetry readings in the sky
where smoking is forbidden
and Jesuits interminably drool
about the good that they have done below
and no poet sings.

LION

Grandpa paced the avenue,
Tired old lion –
Forwards, turn and back
as though with every step
his luggage lightened
as though the years
were falling back
to the hide-and-seek
of childhood

He said he'd die on Wednesday
On Tuesday, a wintry night,
clouds buffeting, no moon,
he took his final walk.
He stopped just once
to pat his pockets
to reassure himself
he'd jetissoned the dross,
shook out his chalk-white mane
and climbed the stairs.

At the funeral my grandma said
"He was a meticulous gentleman."

DOSTOEVSKY'S GRAVE

I am locked in this acropolis
just Feodor and me
I rub my fingers
in his overcoat of stone
gambling my airline ticket
and find in the valley
of my life-line
the gravel of Baden Baden

IN MEMORIAM JOHN JORDAN

We were long on the one bitch road
between the "Hatch" and that "Low" Leeson Street
Haring through Agatha Christie's (you)
Or on some parched afternoon
We'd bump into a waiting moment
With a how d'you do how are you
(As Eddie Maguire used to say)
Or your apocryphal pronouncement
"May God forgive me, all my enemies
Down at one go."

In Grogan's bar with mongering dole-men
Adroop or clattering drunk
The silent country of your endurance
Was something that stepped aside
However insecure the footing
Uninviting the ravines
Conversing with that other John
A Chaplinesque half sided smile
An Oh dear me, to save a fall or two.

After the fireworks have subsided
We will sing old songs
La recherche du temps perdu
And birds will call as though insensed.

DAWN GUEST

My patch of lawn between poplar and oak
Is empty once again. For a moment
In an agony of pride he raised his antlers
Whipped the wind, leapt and was gone.

Perhaps he was never there
Between oak and poplar
This dawn visitor. Too much beauty
Destroys the levels of concentration

But ever since I've watched this patch of grass
As if he still was there – sinews locked for flight
As though we could in one split second
Give skin for skin, muscle for rippling muscle.

Still he lives on in my mind's eye
What I've invested in him
Like an episode of tremendous luck
The pot of gold at the end of the rainbow.

BROTHER

If only he would admit to being born
my brother. Every Christmas, without fail,
a cheque arrives – the nervous cutting of the knife –
it goes up yearly with inflation.
Hastily I post my New Year Card – the feast is over –
clip off another piece of guilt
like breaking off an edge of biscuit.

I know that he'll outlive me
this wombless man. He'll pay
the undertaker, scowl mysteriously
at my friends – a motley crew –
later he'll read my obituary in the press
and find out things he never knew.

HISTORY STOPPED THAT NIGHT

It might have been anyone
but the fact that it was I
who lay in a mulch of leaves
between two ice-ages
watching your face in shadow
speckled like seed-cakes
in a bronze moon-madness, harvest for size
made me wonder at luck that
makes a twist of time
so unimportant. Morning, I woke
a shelf of moss had curled itself into a pillow
it was damp and cold. And you slept deep I think.

History had undone itself like buttons on a coat
We had played farms and families for centuries
of weeping land – gone off – made good or bad
adopted transatlantic ways and accents
become colonial, racist, over sentimental
the hovel of our past made glorious
in the quick buck game and fuck the wogs.

My duty then was to make sure
that he who lay beside me woke that day
though mulch and hypnum might invade
our nostrils all too soon
beneath the forest-floor of someone else's sorrow.

But coming from the hostelry that night
we'd kissed each other flat
and mottled by moon light
fallen like Icarus in history's flight.

LETTER TO MY TEACHER

I am speeding the Esker townland
on my fairy cycle.
I am seven and the day is grained
with a fine Kildare mist.
It is moist as a bull's nose.
I drive my face into it as into a wash-tub,
my neck cools. At the edge of the golf-course
a lorry passes; mud cakes like chocolate
on my socks.

They have thrown me out for writing poems.
Now I am telling you this before I die
I am telling you this in a letter.
Poems were bad they said
so from seven on I knew.
Iris Wellwood you were my teacher,
Iris Wellwood of the sun-red hair,
come all the way from Cavan town
to throw me out for writing poems.

Now I've been thrown out from everywhere
pubs, houses, public transport
and the only reason far's I know
is that frogs keep jumping off the paper
mosquitoes dancing in the cubic yard of my skull
from Leeson Street to Kopovar
from Leningrad on the Nevsky Prospekt
to Clanbrassil Street on the *Villamos*.

You taught me seven nines were sixty-three
but writing poems was a waste of time
I write this letter with sincerest thanks
now that nine times seven years
are nearly gone. I've ridden that fairy bike
a long long way from Esker, Confey or Spion Kop
through the earliest townlands of my mind
the town lands of *Muslin* and *Esther Waters*.

NOTE
for Jacqueline Bardwell

The trouble is I miss the short sea
in an alcove of rock or the wider
more impelling stretch of the Atlantic
I seem to be paralysed between two Drumlins
and the trees against the pewter clouds
unnerve me as though to say "I know your number".

Still at the moment, all is well
and when the time is right
I shall go – there are other places
somewhere with a Russian wind talking down the
    chimney
and the Black Sea breaking wilfully
beyond the reaches of Chekov's garden.

C.T.SCAN

They've put my head inside the big machine.
Jack the cat stalks round my brain.
He purrs, he kneads,
his paws are soft as mushrooms.
He has triumphant eyes.

They talk casually
on the intercom
about stomach pills and airline sickness.

I lie still as stone in this aluminium trunk
thinking of Mary Shelley

A SINGLE ROSE

I have willed my body to the furthering of science
although I'll not be there
to chronicle my findings
I can imagine all the students
pouring over me
"My God, is that a liver?
and those brown cauliflowers are lungs?"
Yes, sir, a fine example of how not to live.
"And what about the brain?"
"Alas the brain. I doubt if this poor sample
ever had one." As with his forceps
he extracts a single rose.

ROSES

My aunt Joyce had the roses
roses of consumption
two round rose buds
blood red roses
roses of consumption
on her cheeks.

In the teeming Mayo rain
every year in the hired house
was when we heard the sea say "Joyce".
We children heard it – "Joyce" –
while the waves dragged back the stones
with a terrifying "oh".

We'd offer her the silence of the mirror
a powder puff, a comb,
and bundled in all kinds of coats
we'd carry her
to Ballycastle, Glenamoy, Belderg or Bunnahowen,
anywhere the sea would growl her name
and she could sit and listen quietly.

But they were cleverer than we
with pills and pillows; in the end a wooden box
they laid her in it like you would a bunch of flowers
in a shoe box – roses maybe
and then we heard the thump of roses
earth and roses – roses
like the blood red roses on her cheeks

THE PRICE OF SHOES IN RUSSIA

I am an old old woman, *Izvinite*
My fingers are nicotine brown
from endless fags. But I exult
in the wings of the choir
that swing from within
the walls of the cathedral.

Till another old old woman,
older even than I, jumps on me
with the speed of hate
cleaves my head with her umbrella
and calls her grandson to evict me.

Being no fool in my eightieth year
I stuff the burning orb into my pocket
Izvinite I am old and stupid as a dog
I beg forgiveness on my hands and knees.
He tells me his name is Yuri.

Yes I'm Yuri – Yuri from Kharkov
And I'm an ancient Protestant woman
from a Catholic country called Ireland
and I wish I'd never smoked
in the precincts of his church.
Oh Yuri, I cry. But Yuri does not beat me.
He sits me down in the mellow shadow of a tree
near the puddled fish pond in the park
and talks of shoes.

Shoes, he says, lighting up,
are very dear in Kharkov.
I take his *Cosmos* gratefully, inhale and cry
Oh yes, but they are also dear in Dublin
Shoes in Dublin are exceptionally dear.

But socks, he cries, we queue for socks
Not to mention stockings I say.

He is shaken with a fine delight
as we work our way up thighwards
and I burn slowly – from inside with a scorching love
from my pocket from the burning cigarette
and from the sun above my double vented skull.

When we embrace we agree to meet in Yalta
and feed cyclamen seeds through the eyelids
of Chekov's dacha.

THE BINGO BUS

In Killinarden there was nothing –
Nothing – but nearer town
there was the Bingo Bus

The Bingo Bus, the Bingo Bus
Nearer to Thee, my God, the Bingo Bus
And *Strip the Willow,* they played
With the driver, trussed the conductor –
Danced *Turkey in the Straw.*

Every Thursday without fail
The ladies rode on the Bingo Bus

And Booze before Bingo and after
And lots of Booze in between
Returning late from Bingo
They ate the conductor whole.

We in Killinarden, wanted, o so much
To have a Bingo Bus of our own

We wrote to the Authorities,
Begged and begged on our knees
T.D.s were hammered, we marched,
Made flags, went on hunger strike
Outside the Dail.

You lot aren't ready for Bingo,
You've only been here a year,
You must have lots more babies
Before you deserve a Bingo Bus.

So every year to the clinic
Three out, one in, four out one in
But still no Bingo Bus

I had to leave Killinarden
Wearied from making flags,
Marching and lobbying and having kids
So I moved right into a hotel.
St. Brendan's is its name

I make sanitary towels for Bingo players
I do my bit for Bingo players
I am on the ball for Bingo players
I'm saving up for Bingo
Saving up for Bingo

LILA'S POTATOES

They asked me to write a poem
about Lila's potatoes
I thought about the eighteen forties
I thought about watercress
I thought about weeds
but they were black
my plants were black
lazy beds, they said, were O.K.

I had spent my life in lazy beds
one way and another – lazy beds
in and out of lazy beds

They'd got me every where
when I slept in different towns,
places, seas, – another child
lazy beds, they said, were O.K. in the famine.

I saw my plants – black – leaves black
stalks black – lazy beds, they said –
in the famine – lazy beds

So I made kids in lazy beds – strapping women
all all from lazy beds – eight altogether
they got jobs in underground London pubs,
strip halls – make-believe – run around
and ended up in lazy beds all eight of them.

Lazy beds make black potatoes – Lila's potatoes
have the blight – lazy beds – Lila's potatoes
they got the blight

Then Seamus took the bad luck out of it
It was the sun, he said, caused it.
I often wondered what caused all my children.
I'm glad it was the sun.

THEMS YOUR MAMMY'S PILLS
for Edward McLachlan

They'd scraped the top soil off the garden
and every step or two they'd hurled a concrete block
bolsters of mud like hippos from the hills
rolled on the planters plantings of the riff-raff of the city.

The schitzophrenic planners had finished off their job
folded their papers, put away their pens –
the city clearances were well ahead.

And all day long a single child was crying
while his father shouted: Don't touch them,
Thems your mammy's pills.

I set to work with zeal to play "Doll's House",
"Doll's life", "Doll's Garden"
while my adolescent sons played "Temporary Heat"
in the living room out front
and drowned the opera of admonitions:
Don't touch them, thems your mammy's pills.

Fragile as needles the women wander forth
laddered with kids, the unborn one ahead
to forge the mile through mud and rut
where mulish earth-removers rest, a crazy sculpture.

They are going back to the city for the day
this is all they live for –
going back to the city for the day.

The line of shops and solitary pub
are camouflaged like check points on the border
the supermarket stretches emptily
a circus of sausages and time
the till-girl gossips in the veg department
Once in a while a woman might come in
to put another pound on
the electronic toy for Christmas.

From behind the curtains every night
the video lights are flickering, butcher blue
Don't touch them thems your mammy's pills.

No one has a job in Killinarden
nowadays they say it is a no go area
I wonder, then, who goes and does not go
in this strange forgotten world
of video and valium

I visited my one time neighbour
not so long ago. She was sitting
in the hangover position
I knew she didn't want to see me
although she'd cried when we were leaving

I went my way
through the quietly rusting motor cars and prams
past the barricades of wire, the harmony of junk.
The babies that I knew are punk-size now
and soon children will have children
and new voices ring the *leit motif:*

Don't touch them, thems your mammy's pills.

AN UNUSUAL IRISH SUMMER
for Nicholas McLachlan

I ask them have they brought the galleys
I am alive and awake with a hole in my head.
My son's face swings above me
like an extraordinary coin
I'd been dreaming of water chestnuts
and the heat beneath my skull
makes me long for that apron of sand
stretching out to the country's eye
in an unusual Irish summer.

KASSIA

Kassia, the 9th century Byzantine poet
wore epigrams like bangles on her arms
when offered marriage with the emperor
she scalded him with wit.

Banished from the court
Columns of stone will kneel
she said, before you change a fool.

A learned fool, God save us.
The pigs are eating pearls.

SKIPPING BANVILLE IN BARCELONA
for Colm Tóibín

I am infinitely caused
beneath the pinnacles of Gaudi
Mesmerising struts, angels,
apostles, dog-lion
timber and stone
"There are no straight lines
in nature" Gaudi said.

The quilted edifice towers
twin pinnacles (God can only
see downwards) religious
phalluses – bourgeois trinkets
gingerbread and wine

Retiring afterwards to remember
and cool down I pick up the Book of Evidence
watch Carmen being murdered once again
remember previous jealousies and loves
and spend the evening
skipping Banville in Barcelona.

MAGGIE'S COTTAGE
for Geraldine Whelan

There we kept time pressed apart
like a row of books supported by two book-ends
there we erased the pitch and toss
of all the lives we'd lived –
the pot holes of disaster.

The "where oh where" of now is the question of that time
when as Vladimir and Estragon we walked the avenue
with our water bottles of laughter, our occasional fights
We flew saucers of friendship above the stars
which landed in the lap of the "big house"
as when dawn brought the demon Harding to cook our
breakfast complete with pike and hangover.

If the snake of time has shed its skin again
I know that artichokes are different from thistles.
We left our marks – a painted room – a broken pane of glass
a hedge of beans a colony of spinach.

Leland Bardwell grew up in Leixlip, Co Kildare. She has lived in London, Paris, and Dublin. At present living in County Monaghan. She went to school in Dublin and later studied Ancient History in London University as an extra-mural student. She has given poetry readings all over Ireland, France, Hungary and England. She was awarded a creative writing bursary by the Irish Arts Council in 1978 and again in 1980. She has worked as a translator in Paris and Budapest. She is also a novelist and a playwright.

Her publications include:
poetry: "The Mad Cyclist" (New Writers Press 1970)
    "The Fly and the Bed Bug" (Beaver Row Press 1984)

novels: "Girl on a Bicycle" (Irish Writers Co-op 1976)
    "That London Winter" (Irish Writers Co-op 1981)
    "The House"   (Brandon 1984)
    "There We Have Been" (Attic 1989)

Short stories: "Different Kinds of Love" (Ullstein, Berlin 1991)

stage plays: "Thursday", Trinity College 1973
            "Open Ended Prescription" Peacock 1979
            "Life of Edith Piaf" Olympia 1984